The Adventures of Scuba Jack
Copyright 2021 by Beth Costanzo

CUTTING PRACTICE

CUTTING PRACTICE

CUTOUTS

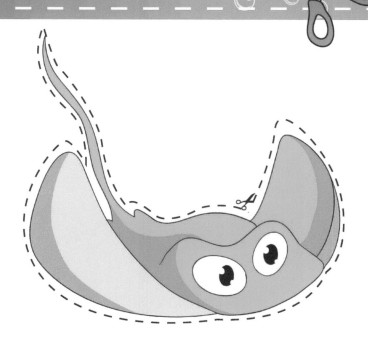

CUTOUTS

OCEAN PUZZLE
Cut and assemble

1   2   3   4   5

OCEAN PUZZLE
Cut and assemble

1   2   3   4   5

OCEAN PUZZLE

Cut and assemble

1   2   3   4   5

4   3   5   2   1

OCEAN PUZZLE

Cut and assemble

1   2   3   4   5

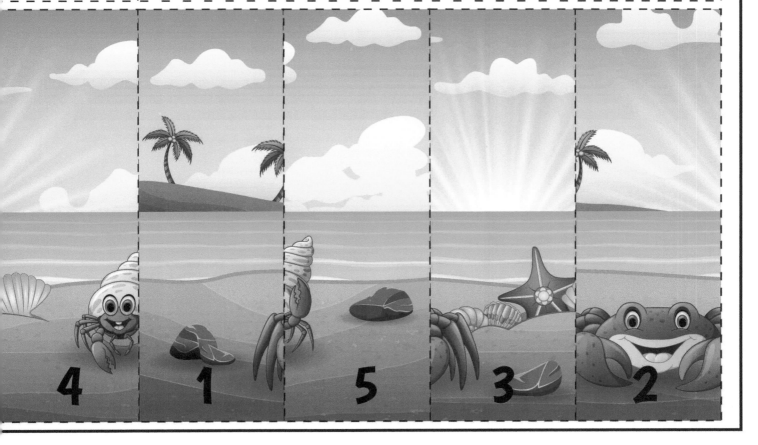

4   1   5   3   2

OCEAN PUZZLE
Cut and assemble

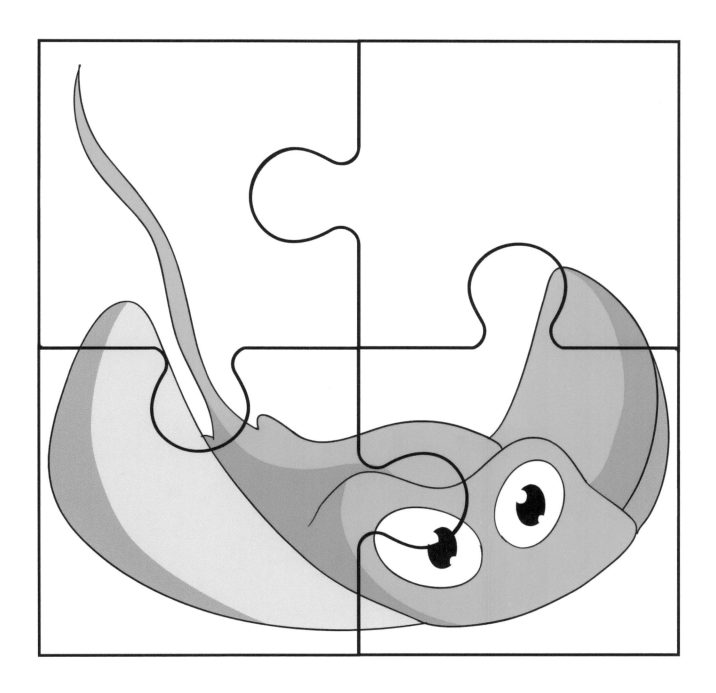

OCEAN PUZZLE
Cut and assemble

OCEAN PUZZLE
Cut and assemble

OCEAN PUZZLE
Cut and assemble

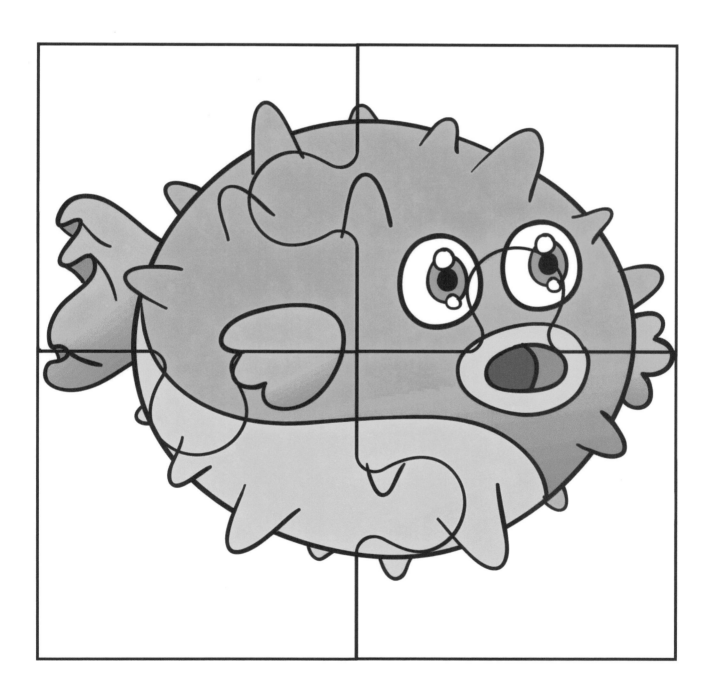

OCEAN PUZZLE
Cut and assemble

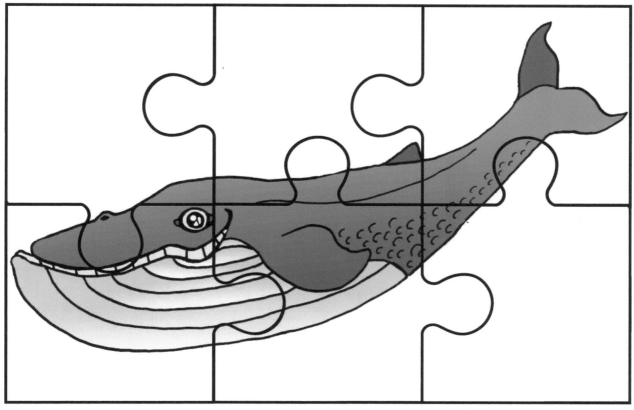

CRAB CRAFT
Cut and glue them on their place

TURTLE CRAFT
Cut and glue them on their place

FISH CRAFT
Cut and glue them on their place

SEAL CRAFT

Cut and glue them on their place

Visit us at:

www.adventuresofscubajack.com

Printed in the USA
CPSIA information can be obtained
at www.ICGtesting.com
LVHW061516061223
765842LV00002B/9